How to Reach Your Favorite Sports Star

by
Larry Strauss

Lowell House Juvenile
Los Angeles
• • • • • •
Contemporary Books
Chicago

ISBN: 1-56565-201-0

10 9 8 7 6 5 4 3 2 1

Reach out and get in touch with someone!

*Y*our favorite athletes work hard to perform to the best of their abilities—and they love to hear that you appreciate their efforts. If you've ever had the impulse to tell a special sports celeb exactly how you feel, now is the time to do it!

But how do you reach your favorite sports star? This book will show you how. So read about your favorite athletes in the following pages, then get out your stationery and write on! And remember these pointers for best results:

➤ If you want a reply, it's best to send a self-addressed, stamped envelope (SASE)—an envelope that is stamped with the proper postage and has your own name and address printed legibly on it—along with your letter.

➤ If you are writing to or from a country other than the United States (for instance, if you are in Canada and writing to a star at a U.S. address), you will need international postage coupons, because a simple SASE won't work in other countries. By including the postage coupons, which are available at any post office, you'll have a better chance of receiving a reply.

➤ Not all celebrities have fan clubs. When you send your letter you might want to request fan club information—or, if you feel like you've got the time and devotion, you could inquire about setting up a fan club for that star yourself!

➤ Always remember that sports stars change addresses just like anybody else. They move, train in various places for months, or change teams. But the addresses included in this book are stable, so even if the person you write to decides to move, your letter will probably be forwarded to the new address.

➤ Have fun! Letter writing is a great way to express yourself to people you care about, and athletes love to hear from their fans!

Contents

▼▼▼▼▼▼▼▼▼▼▼▼▼▼▼▼

Jim Abbott

■ ■ ■ ■ ■ ■ ■ ■ ■ ■ ■ ■ ■ ■ ■ ■ ■

*B*y now, most people know that Jim Abbott is the first major league pitcher in history with only one hand. Millions have watched his amazing delivery: He rests his glove on the end of his right arm, goes into his windup, throws, and then with lightning speed slips the mitt onto his left hand so that he can field the ball. At every level of play—from Little League through high school and college—Jim has received admiration for his hard work and determination.

Vital Stats

➤ Height: 6'3"
➤ Weight: 210
➤ Bats: left-handed
➤ Throws: left-handed
➤ Birthplace: Flint, Michigan
➤ Other sport: Jim was a high school football star.
➤ In his spare time: enjoys swimming, riding a boogie board, reading, and spending time with his wife

Cool Credits

➤ Sullivan Award (best amateur athlete), 1988
➤ Most Valuable Player of University of Michigan baseball team, 1988
➤ Sporting News All-American College Baseball team, 1988
➤ Big Ten Conference MVP, 1988
➤ Olympic gold medal (pitched gold medal game against Japan), 1988
➤ Topps all-rookie selection, 1989

4

Birthday Beat
September 19, 1967

So You Want to Know—
One of Jim's major accomplishments? Jim never played minor league baseball. He went straight from the University of Michigan Wolverines to the Olympics to the California Angels. He is the fifteenth player in baseball history to go straight to the majors, bypassing the minor leagues.

Jim Abbott
c/o The New York Yankees
Yankee Stadium
Bronx, NY 10451

Andre Agassi

Cool Credits

➤ U.S. Clay Court Championships winner, 1988
➤ French Open finalist, 1990, 1991
➤ Wimbledon winner, 1992
➤ Davis Cup winning team, 1992
➤ Top 10 ranking, 1988–1993

Birthday Beat

April 29, 1970

Vital Stats

➤ Height: 5'11"
➤ Weight: 175
➤ Birthplace: Las Vegas, Nevada
➤ Current residence: Las Vegas, Nevada
➤ Motorcycle mania: has his own custom-made Harley Davidson with a built-in stereo and TV!
➤ Collects: cars (he has over twenty-five!)

He is famous for his TV commercials advertising cameras, even to people who have never seen a tennis match. In those commercials he says, "Image is everything." But there is much more to Andre Agassi than image. He is a hardworking, very talented young tennis star. He has been a pro since the age of sixteen and a perennial Top 10 star since age eighteen. Andre has endured slumps and tough losses and has shown that he is not just another pretty face.

So You Want to Know—

How Andre got into tennis? When he was an infant, his father tied a tennis ball over his crib. Then when Andre was a little over a year old, his father used to put a Ping-Pong paddle in his hand and toss balloons at him. By the time Andre was two, he could serve on a regulation tennis court.

Andre Agassi
International Management Group
One Erieview Plaza
Cleveland, OH 44114

Troy Aikman

▼▼▼▼▼▼▼▼▼▼▼▼▼▼▼▼▼▼▼▼

*H*e may not be the best quarterback in football—not yet, anyway—but Troy Aikman has already proven that he is one of the toughest. As a child, he had to wear casts up to his knees to correct a deformity in his feet. As a football player, he's also had his share of challenges. His first pro season, the Dallas Cowboys were 1-15, and Troy had to fight with Steve Walsh for the starting quarterback job. But he hung in there and never gave up. For three years, he and the Cowboys continued to get better, and in Super Bowls XXVII and XXVIII, Troy led the Cowboys to victory.

So You Want to Know—

Troy's little-known honor? There is a street named after him. Called Troy Aikman Avenue, the street lies in Henryetta, Oklahoma, where Troy's family moved when he was twelve.

Cool Credits

➤ NCAA all-American, 1989
➤ First NFL draft pick, 1989
➤ Threw a record eighty-nine post-season passes without an interception, 1992–1993
➤ Super Bowl victory, 1993, 1994
➤ Super Bowl Most Valuable Player, 1993

Birthday Beat
November 21, 1966

Vital Stats
➤ Height: 6'4"
➤ Weight: 217
➤ Birthplace: West Covina, California

➤ Current residence: Irving, Texas
➤ College: University of California, Los Angeles
➤ Majored in: economics
➤ Leg power: can lift 640 pounds with his legs!
➤ Nickname: T-Roy

Troy Aikman
c/o Dallas Cowboys
One Cowboy's Parkway
Irving, TX 75063

Oksana Baiul

■ ■ ■ ■ ■ ■ ■ ■ ■ ■ ■ ■ ■ ■ ■ ■

*O*ksana Baiul has overcome many hardships before getting to where she is today. When she was thirteen years old, she lost her mother to cancer and, shortly after that, her skating coach of nine years moved to Canada. The world-class skating coach, Galina Zmierskaya, became Oksana's coach as well as her surrogate mother.

With Zmierskaya's help and Oksana's own talent, in 1993, Oksana won the World Championships in her first-ever international competition. Most recently, she won the gold medal at the 1994 Winter Olympics, just inching out Nancy Kerrigan.

Vital Stats

➤ Height: 5'2"
➤ Weight: 102
➤ Birthplace: Dnepropetrovsk, Ukraine
➤ Current residence: Odessa, Ukraine

➤ In her spare time: loves to crank up the music of Hammer and Dr. Alban, and dance, dance, dance!
➤ Favorite type of story: fairy tales. She loves *The Little Mermaid*, *Aladdin*, and *Beauty and the Beast*. Her favorite book is a Russian fairy tale about a crooked horse.
➤ Favorite ice skater: three-time U.S. Champion and 1990 World Champion Jill Trenary

So You Want to Know—

How Oksana got into figure skating? When Oksana was only three years old, her grandfather gave her her first pair of ice skates in the hopes that she might lose some weight and eventually study ballet. While she did not commit herself to ballet for a profession, Oksana does incorporate ballet and other dance moves into all her skating routines.

Birthday Beat
November 16, 1977

Cool Credits

➤ Placed second in European Championships, 1993
➤ Placed first in World Championships, 1993
➤ Placed first at Skate America, 1993
➤ Place second in European Championships, 1994
➤ Olympic gold medal, 1994

Oksana Baiul
U.S. Figure Skating Association
20 First St.
Colorado Springs, CO 80906

Charles Barkley

❑ ❑ ❑ ❑ ❑ ❑ ❑ ❑ ❑ ❑ ❑ ❑ ❑ ❑ ❑ ❑ ❑ ❑

*A*s a high school sophomore basketball player, Charles Barkley used to boast that he would one day make it to the NBA. No one believed him, because he couldn't even make the varsity team. But Charles worked overtime on his game and never stopped believing in himself. At six feet six inches, he is shorter than some guards, yet he pulls down more rebounds than many centers.

After some tough seasons with the Philadelphia 76ers, he was traded to the Phoenix Suns in 1992 and has helped to make them one of the very best teams in the league. Later that year, he made the Olympic 1992 Dream Team and was recognized as one of the twelve best basketball players in the world.

Cool Credits

➤ NCAA Southeast Conference Player of the Year, 1983
➤ Fifth overall in 1984 NBA draft
➤ All-rookie team, 1985
➤ All-star team every year, 1986–1994
➤ All-NBA first team, 1988–1991
➤ Olympic gold medal, 1992
➤ NBA Most Valuable Player, 1993

Vital Stats

➤ Height: 6'6"
➤ Weight: 250
➤ Birthplace: Leeds, Alabama
➤ Current residence: Phoenix, Arizona
➤ Nicknames: The Round Mound of Rebound, Sir Charles

So You Want to Know—

How powerful Charles is? On his twenty-second birthday, during a game, Barkley dunked a ball so hard that it moved the basket support (which weighs 2,240 pounds) six inches.

➤ In his spare time: watches soap operas, especially "The Young and the Restless"
➤ Favorite pet: After each home game, Charles relaxes in his Jacuzzi with his little yellow rubber duck.

Birthday Beat

February 20, 1963

Charles Barkley
c/o Phoenix Suns
P.O. Box 1369
Phoenix, AZ 85001

Bonnie Blair

▼▼▼▼▼▼▼▼▼▼▼▼▼▼▼▼▼

*A*lthough it does not get as much attention as many other sports, speed skating is an exciting and very challenging international event. It takes great speed as well as agility to be a champion. Bonnie Blair has all that and more. She is a great competitor, winning her first speed-skating race when she was four years old. When she finished eighth during the 1984 Winter Olympics, Bonnie was amazed by the speed of her competitors, but at the same time vowed to defeat them next time. And in 1988 and 1992 (and 1994!) she did.

Vital Stats

➤ Height: 5'4"
➤ Weight: 130
➤ Birthplace: Cornwall, New York

➤ Current residence: Champaign, Illinois
➤ In her spare time: reads romance novels
➤ Top speed on skates: 35 miles per hour
➤ Memorable song: When Bonnie won her 1992 gold medal, her family sang "My Bonnie Lies Over the Ocean."
➤ Favorite sandwich: peanut butter and jelly

Birthday Beat

March 18, 1964

So You Want to Know—

One of Bonnie's claims to fame? Bonnie may not be the most famous athlete in the United States, but she is very well known in one part of the country. Her face appears on a postage stamp in St. Thomas, one of the U.S. Virgin Islands in the Caribbean Sea.

Cool Credits

➤ Olympic gold medal in the 500 meters, 1988, 1992, 1994

➤ Olympic gold medal in the 1,000 meters, 1992, 1994

➤ Only American woman ever to win gold in three consecutive Olympics

➤ Only woman in the world to win the 500-meter speed-skating event three Olympics in a row

Bonnie Blair
Advantage International, Inc.
1025 Thomas Jefferson St., NW
Washington, D.C. 20007

Jim Courier

So You Want to Know—

One of Jim's most famous fans? During the opening ceremony of the 1992 Olympics, NBA star Charles Barkley pushed a French athlete out of the way in order to get his picture taken with Jim Courier.

Cool Credits

➤ U.S. Open finalist, 1991
➤ Ranked first in the world, 1991
➤ French Open winner, 1991, 1992
➤ Australian Open winner, 1992, 1993
➤ French Open finalist, 1993
➤ Wimbledon finalist, 1993

■ ■ ■ ■ ■ ■ ■ ■ ■ ■ ■ ■

Jim Courier isn't the first American men's tennis star to reach the number one ranking in the world, but he's the first to do it since John McEnroe in 1985. And with the world of tennis too competitive to be dominated by any one player, a stint at the top is quite an accomplishment. For Jim it is the result of hard work and a no-quit attitude. Even if he's down to the last point in the last set of the match, he never loses his determination to make a comeback.

Vital Stats

➤ Height: 6'1"
➤ Weight: 170
➤ Birthplace: Sanford, Florida
➤ Current residence: Palm Desert, California
➤ Hits: right-handed
➤ Backstroke: two-handed

➤ In his spare time: spends time with his girlfriend, studies French, plays the Fender Stratocaster guitar and drums

Birthday Beat

August 17, 1970

Jim Courier
International Management Group
One Erieview Plaza
Cleveland, OH 44144

17

Randall Cunningham

□ □ □ □ □ □ □ □ □ □ □ □ □

*G*rowing up in sunny Santa Barbara, California, quarterback Randall Cunningham had all year to practice football outdoors. In 1985, he moved to Pennsylvania to play for the Philadelphia Eagles, and today he is considered one of the most dangerous scoring threats in the NFL. He can pass in the pocket, he can scramble and throw on the run, and he can rush for big yardage. He can even punt when his team needs him to. Randall has yet to reach the Super Bowl, but he has managed to take a team that was near the bottom of the league and make it a consistent contender.

Cool Credits

➤ As quarterback for the University of Nevada, Las Vegas, he became the third QB in NCAA history to pass for more than 2,500 yards for three consecutive seasons.

➤ Pro Bowl Most Valuable Player, 1989
➤ Holds team record of forty-three completions out of forty-six pass attempts in a game, 1989

Birthday Beat
March 27, 1963

So You Want to Know—

About Randall's famous brother? Randall is the younger brother of a former NFL star: New England Patriots fullback Sam "Bam" Cunningham. In fact, older brother Sam bought his parents the house where Randall grew up.

Vital Stats

➤ Height: 6'4"
➤ Weight: 193
➤ Birthplace: Santa Barbara, California
➤ Position: quarterback
➤ Throws: right-handed
➤ In his spare time: hosts his own local TV talk show

Randall Cunningham
c/o Scrambler Incorporated
110 Marter Ave., Suite 408
Moorestown, NJ 08057

Clyde Drexler

▼▼▼▼▼▼▼▼▼▼▼▼▼▼▼▼▼▼▼▼

*I*n college, Clyde Drexler and Hakeem Olajuwan were part of what became known as "Phi-Slamma-Jamma," the explosive University of Houston Cougars, who went to the Final Four two years in a row. As a pro, Clyde helped the Portland Trail Blazers' rise from the NBA basement to the penthouse. They have reached the finals two out of three years and established themselves as one of the NBA's best teams. Clyde has experienced his share of "almosts" and other disappointments in his basketball career, but he has maintained a positive outlook and camaraderie not only with his teammates but with all pro ball players.

Cool Credits

➤ Helped Houston Cougars reach two consecutive NCAA Final Fours, 1982, 1983
➤ NBA all-rookie team, 1984
➤ NBA Western Conference all-star team, 1986–1994
➤ All-NBA second team, 1988, 1991
➤ NBA finals, 1990, 1992
➤ All-NBA first team, 1992
➤ First runner-up for NBA's Most Valuable Player, 1992
➤ 1992 Olympic Dream Team member

Birthday Beat
June 22, 1962

So You Want to Know—

How Clyde proved he was one of the best jumpers in basketball? He once dunked a basketball into an eleven-foot, seven-inch basket just to show that he could do it!

Vital Stats

➤ Height: 6'7"
➤ Weight: 222
➤ Birthplace: New Orleans, Louisiana
➤ Current residence: Portland, Oregon
➤ College: University of Houston

➤ In his spare time: plays tennis and golf
➤ Nickname: Clyde the Glide
➤ Favorite foods: red beans and rice
➤ Favorite movie: *Sarafina!*

Clyde Drexler
700 N.E. Multnomah St.
Lloyd Building, Suite 600
Portland, OR 97232

John Elway

▪ ▪ ▪ ▪ ▪ ▪ ▪ ▪ ▪ ▪ ▪ ▪ ▪ ▪ ▪

John Elway is one of the most dangerous offensive players to ever put on shoulder pads. This big quarterback can throw from in or out of the pocket. He can escape defensive rushers and run for big gains—or stop suddenly and throw a bullet pass to an open receiver. Some have called John the best natural athlete to ever play quarterback. He has led the Denver Broncos to become consistent Super Bowl contenders.

- Super Bowl appearances, 1987, 1988, 1990
- Only quarterback ever to pass for 3,000 yards and rush for 400 in a single season

Vital Stats

- Height: 6'3"
- Weight: 215
- Birthplace: Port Angeles, Washington
- Current residence: Aurora, Colorado
- Upper body strength: can lift 330 pounds
- In his spare time: plays golf, plays with his kids
- Other ventures: owns his own car lot in Denver

Birthday Beat

June 28, 1960

Cool Credits

- All-American for Stanford University, 1980, 1982
- First draft pick NFL, 1983

John Elway
c/o Denver Broncos
5700 Logan St.
Denver, CO 80216

Janet Evans

*B*y the age of seventeen Janet Evans had become one of the greatest swimmers of all time. She also had a lot of grown-up decisions to make. For one thing, she had to decide whether to be a student athlete or to accept the big money endorsements she was being offered in the aftermath of her three Olympic gold medals in 1988. Janet opted to be a student, and while she swam for Stanford University, she maintained a 3.4 grade point average. When Janet's body began to mature and change, she had more questions to answer: Could she be a champion with a woman's body? Would she still have that lightning fast start and powerful windmill stroke? Janet answered that question with three medals in the 1992 Olympics!

Cool Credits

➤ U.S. Nationals first place 400-meter freestyle, 800-meter freestyle, and 400-meter individual medley, 1987

➤ World's record in the 800-meter freestyle, 1989, and the 1500-meter freestyle and 400-meter freestyle, 1988

➤ Olympic gold medals 400-meter freestyle, 400-meter individual medley, and 800-meter freestyle, 1988

➤ Sullivan Award (best amateur athlete), 1989

► World Championships gold medal 400-meter freestyle and 800-meter freestyle, 1991
► Olympic silver medal 400-meter freestyle, 1992
► Olympic gold medal 4x100-meter freestyle relay, 1992
► Olympic gold medal 800-meter freestyle, 1992

Birthday Beat
August 28, 1971

Vital Stats

► Height: 5'6"
► Weight: 113
► Birthplace: Fullerton, California
► Current residence: Austin, Texas
► In her spare time: loves to garden around her apartment, and go dancing, to the movies, and shopping; also a whiz on the piano

So You Want to Know—

When Janet started swimming? Janet began working out in the pool before she was two years old. Her mother remembers Janet swimming laps at the YMCA, then getting out and asking for her bottle and a fresh diaper.

Janet Evans
U.S. Swimming
One Olympic Plaza
Colorado Springs, CO 80909

Patrick Ewing

▼▼▼▼▼▼▼▼▼▼▼▼▼▼▼▼▼▼▼

P atrick Ewing did not play basketball growing up on the island country of Jamaica, where the main sports are soccer (which they call football) and cricket. He was thirteen years old when he immigrated, along with his parents, to Massachusetts. One day he was walking past a playground and was asked to join a basketball game. He wasn't very good, but he enjoyed the game and decided to get better at it. And he did. By the time Patrick graduated from Latin High School, in Cambridge, Massachusetts, he was one of the best high school hoopsters in the nation. At Georgetown University, four years later, he was the best college senior basketball player in the country, and today, he is one of the best basketball players in the world.

Cool Credits

➤ NCAA championship with Georgetown, 1984
➤ Number one overall in 1985 NBA draft
➤ Olympic gold medal, 1984, 1992
➤ All-star team, 1985–1994
➤ All-NBA first team, 1990

Vital Stats

➤ Height: 7'0"
➤ Weight: 240
➤ Birthplace: Kingston, Jamaica
➤ Current residence: Potomac, Maryland, and Fort Lee, New Jersey
➤ In his spare time: listens to reggae music and the blues, watches boxing and football

➤ Nickname: Beast of the East
➤ Favorite foods: curried goat and other Jamaican specialties
➤ Childhood idol: world-famous soccer star Pelé

Birthday Beat

August 5, 1962

Patrick Ewing
c/o The New York Knicks
4 Penn Plaza
New York, NY 10001

Steffi Graf

*O*nly five people in the history of tennis have won the Grand Slam—victories at the Australian Open, French Open, Wimbledon, and the U.S. Open in the same year. Steffi Graf is the most recent of those five, winning the Grand Slam in 1988 at age nineteen. There is nothing fancy about the way she plays. Her serve is explosive and the rest of her game is powerful.

Steffi started playing tennis in her parents' basement, hitting a ball over a piece of string tied between two chairs. By the time she was thirteen, she was good enough for the women's pro circuit. She couldn't beat anyone but she never gave up, and in 1986 she started winning. And winning. And winning.

Cool Credits

➤ French Open winner, 1987, 1988
➤ U.S. Open winner, 1988, 1989, 1993
➤ Olympic gold medal, 1988
➤ Wimbledon winner, 1988, 1989, 1991, 1992, 1993
➤ Australian Open winner, 1988–1990, 1993
➤ Volkswagen Cup winner, 1991
➤ BMW European Indoor Tournament winner, 1991
➤ Olympic silver medal, 1992

Vital Stats

➤ Height: 5'9"
➤ Weight: 130
➤ Hits: right-handed
➤ Birthplace: Mannheim, Germany
➤ Current residences: Brühl, Germany, and Delray Beach, Florida
➤ In her spare time: loves reading (especially Stephen King novels), shopping, going to the movies, listening to rock music (especially Phil Collins and Bruce Springsteen), playing cards, and collecting T-shirts
➤ Pets: two German shepherds, Max and Zar, and a boxer named Ben

Birthday Beat

June 14, 1969

So You Want to Know—

How famous Steffi is? Steffi is known all over the world, but in Germany, her home, she isn't just well known—she's a national hero! In fact, in a survey more Germans recognized her than the country's leader, Chancellor Helmut Kohl.

Steffi Graf
Advantage International
1025 Thomas Jefferson St., NW
Washington, D.C. 20007

Wayne Gretzky

*A*s far as hockey players go, Wayne Gretzky is not very big and does not have much physical strength. But he is tough, and he is arguably the greatest player in the game of hockey. His notoriety as a hockey player began when he joined a league for ten-year-olds. In 85 games he scored 378 goals. By the time he was seventeen, he'd become good enough to turn professional. In his first season in the World Hockey League, Wayne was Rookie of the Year. In his first season in the NHL, he scored an amazing 137 points on 51 goals and 86 assists. During the next eight years, he and the Edmonton Oilers dominated the NHL. In 1988, he was traded to the Los Angeles Kings, and during the following season he became the all-time NHL scoring leader. Four seasons later, in 1993, Wayne helped the Kings to their first-ever Stanley Cup finals.

Birthday Beat
January 26, 1961

Vital Stats
➤ Height: 5'11"
➤ Weight: 170
➤ Birthplace: Brantford, Ontario (Canada)

➤ Nicknames: The Great One, Gretz
➤ Hobby: breeds and races thoroughbred horses

Cool Credits

➤ All-time NHL scoring leader
➤ All-time NHL goals record
➤ League leader in goals four times
➤ League leader in assists twelve times
➤ Nine-time NHL Most Valuable Player (more than any other player)
➤ Has won four Stanley Cups (with the Edmonton Oilers)
➤ Played on eight NHL all-star teams

So You Want to Know—

About Wayne's interest in football? He and his wife, Janet, are part owners of the Toronto Argonauts, who play for the Canadian Football League.

Wayne Gretzky
c/o Michael Barnett
International Management Group
11755 Wilshire Blvd., Suite 850
Los Angeles, CA 90025

Florence Griffith Joyner

▼▼▼▼▼▼▼▼▼▼▼▼▼▼

So You Want to Know—

About Flo-Jo's connections with pro basketball? She never hit the court as a team member, but rather as a clothing designer! In 1989, she designed the new uniforms for the Indiana Pacers.

Birthday Beat

December 21, 1959

Vital Stats

➤ Height: 5'8"
➤ Weight: 130
➤ Birthplace: Mojave Desert, California
➤ Current residence: Newport Beach, California
➤ In her spare time: loves designing her own clothes, collecting antique dolls, playing with her pet snake
➤ Nickname: Flo-Jo
➤ In Hollywood: appeared on the sitcom "227" as herself

Cool Credits

➤ Olympic silver medal 100 meters, 1984
➤ Olympic gold medals 100 meters, 200 meters, and 4x100-meter relay, 1988
➤ Jesse Owens Award (year's outstanding track-and-field athlete), 1988
➤ Sullivan Award (best amateur athlete), 1988

*W*orld-class sprinters usually aren't world famous. But Florence Griffith Joyner has made a big name for herself. She has had as many commercial endorsements as some NBA and major league baseball stars. Florence grew up in Los Angeles, but used to visit her father who lived in the California desert. She spent time chasing jackrabbits, which helped her to develop her great speed. These days, she may not look like the fastest woman runner in the world with her ultrafashionable clothes and long, artistically painted nails. But don't let that fool you. She's a world record holder and an Olympic champion with the perfect combination of speed and grace.

➤ Tass (Soviet Press Agency) Athlete of the Year, 1988

➤ U.S. Olympic Committee Award, 1989

➤ Golden Camera Award, 1989

➤ Women's world record for 100 meters (10.49 seconds), 1988

Florence Griffith Joyner
c/o Gordon Baskin & Associates
11444 West Olympic Blvd., 10th floor
Los Angeles, CA 90064

Rickey Henderson

Rickey Henderson is the consummate leadoff hitter. He can hit with power or finesse, and he consistently has a high batting average and on-base percentage. Once he gets on base, he is a pitcher's and catcher's nightmare—the game's all-time base stealer. Even if he doesn't steal a base, he is enough of a distraction to cause problems for the pitcher and help out the next man at the plate. Always one to make things happen, Rickey is one of the most exciting major leaguers to watch.

Cool Credits

➤ Only rookie to steal 100 bases in a single season

➤ Single-season record for leadoff home runs (6)

➤ Stole 130 bases in one season, surpassing Lou Brock's single-season stolen-base record (118), 1982

➤ Shattered Lou Brock's career stolen base record (938), 1991

Vital Stats

➤ Height: 5'10"
➤ Weight: 190
➤ Birthplace: Chicago, Illinois
➤ Current residence: Hillsborough, California
➤ Position: outfield
➤ Bats: left-handed
➤ In his spare time: watches soap operas and listens to music, especially Luther Vandross

Birthday Beat

December 25, 1958

So You Want to Know—

About Rickey's *football* career? Rickey Henderson was an all-American high school football player, rushing for 1,100 yards during his senior year. He was offered college football scholarships from USC and UCLA at the same time the Oakland A's offered him a baseball contract. His mother influenced him to play baseball because there was less chance of injury and he would be able to play longer.

Rickey Henderson
c/o Toronto Blue Jays
Skydome
300 Bremner Blvd., Suite 3200
Toronto, Ontario
Canada M5V 383

Bo Jackson

So You Want to Know—

One of Bo's ambitions? In addition to everything "Bo knows," he wants to get to know the skies. He plans to one day get a pilot's license and fly World War II fighter planes.

Birthday Beat

November 30, 1962

Cool Credits

➤ First three-sport letterman (baseball, football, and track) in Southeastern Collegiate Conference history
➤ Heisman Trophy winner, 1985
➤ First Kansas City Royals player ever to hit at least twenty-five home runs and steal at least twenty-five bases in one season, 1988
➤ All-star baseball game Most Valuable Player, 1989

□ □ □ □ □ □ □ □ □ □ □ □ □ □ □ □ □ □

Many have said it could not be done—to have simultaneous baseball and football careers. Some athletes have played more than one sport, but never in the same year. But for Bo Jackson, it was both the diamond and the gridiron. Doubters expected him to falter in one or both sports as he played baseball for the Kansas City Royals and football for the Los Angeles Raiders. He kept getting better each season, until injuries suddenly and abruptly stopped both careers. Bo has since recovered and is miraculously back in baseball, hitting home runs and stealing bases with regularity.

Vital Stats

➤ Height: 6'1"
➤ Weight: 225
➤ Birthplace: Bessemer, Alabama
➤ Current residence: Leawood, Kansas

➤ In his spare time: hunts, fishes, and enjoys archery
➤ His real name: Vincent Edward Jackson
➤ Favorite food: catfish
➤ College: Auburn University

Bo Jackson
c/o California Angels
Anaheim Stadium
Anaheim, CA 92803

Larry Johnson

He always looked older than he was—and he played that way, too. When he was a freshman in high school, Larry Johnson told his coach that he could start on the varsity basketball team, and he was right. When he was in college, Larry played like a pro. Now after only a few seasons in the pros, he plays like a veteran star. He can do it all: shoot, rebound, handle the ball, and play tough defense. He has strength, speed, quickness, and determination. Larry is one of the league's new stars, and no one knows yet how far he will rise.

Vital Stats

➤ Height: 6'7"
➤ Weight: 250
➤ Birthplace: Tyler, Texas
➤ Current residences: Dallas, Texas, and Lake Wylie, North Carolina
➤ College: University of Nevada, Las Vegas
➤ In his spare time: likes to visit his old neighborhood in south Dallas, listen to music, and cruise in his four-wheel drive
➤ Nickname: Grandma (from the sneaker commercials where he plays the part of his own grandmother slam-dunking a basketball)

Cool Credits

➤ Junior College Player of the Year (Odessa Junior College), 1988, 1989
➤ NCAA National Championship with the University of Nevada, Las Vegas, 1990

> ➤ Number one draft pick by the Charlotte Hornets, 1991

> ➤ NCAA Player of the Year, 1991

> ➤ NBA Rookie of the Year, 1992

> ➤ NBA Eastern Conference all-star team, 1993, 1994

> ➤ Led expansion team Charlotte Hornets to their first playoff appearance, 1993

Birthday Beat

March 14, 1969

So You Want to Know—

How strong Larry is? It is one thing to tear down a rim from an NBA backboard; they are made to come down under a certain amount of weight. But the rims in city parks are made to stay on, no matter what. Yet, when he was a teenager, playing on his favorite sandlot basketball court in south Dallas, Larry went up for a slam dunk one time and jammed with such strength that he came down with the rim in his hand.

Larry Johnson
c/o Charlotte Hornets
2 First Union Center
Suite 2600
Charlotte, NC 28282

Michael Jordan

■ ■ ■ ■ ■ ■ ■ ■ ■ ■ ■ ■ ■

Some have called Michael Jordan the best all-around athlete ever to play basketball; others just flat out say he was the greatest hoopster of all time. He accomplished every goal imaginable for a basketball player—an NCAA championship, three consecutive NBA titles, scoring titles, Most Valuable Player awards. Now, with nothing left to prove on the court, Michael has retired from basketball and has joined the Chicago White Sox baseball team.

So You Want to Know—

Michael's plans for the future? After he became a pro basketball player for the Chicago Bulls, Michael Jordan started playing golf. Now he loves golf so much that he wants to become a professional golfer— maybe after he retires from another love: baseball!

Vital Stats

➤ Height: 6'6"
➤ Weight: 198
➤ Birthplace: Brooklyn, New York
➤ Current residence: Northbrook, Illinois
➤ In his spare time: plays golf and billiards, bowls, watches stock car races
➤ Nickname: Air Jordan

Cool Credits

➤ NCAA Championship with the University of North Carolina
➤ Drafted third overall in 1984 NBA draft

➤ Olympic gold medals, 1984, 1992
➤ Rookie of the Year, 1985
➤ All-star team 1985, 1987–1993
➤ NBA Most Valuable Player, 1988, 1991, 1992, 1993
➤ NBA all-defensive team 1987–1993
➤ NBA Championship, 1991–1993

Birthday Beat

February 17, 1963

Michael Jordan
c/o Barbara Allen
ProServ Basketball and Football
5335 Wisconsin Ave., NW, Suite 850
Washington, D.C. 20015

or try:
Air Jordan Flight Club
Ryan Morland
One Bowerman Dr.
Beaverton, OR 97005

Jackie Joyner-Kersee

*T*here are great athletes, and there are great all-around athletes. Jackie Joyner-Kersee is definitely a great all-around athlete. Just as the decathlon determines the best male athlete, Jackie's event, the heptathlon (seven different track-and-field events), determines the best female athlete in the world. Jackie can run long and medium distances, and can do the high jump, long jump, hurdles, and more. She dominated the heptathlon throughout much of the 1980s, winning Olympic and other international competition medals and setting a world's record of 7,291 points.

So You Want to Know—

How Jackie and Flo-Jo are related? Jackie's brother, Al Joyner, was Florence Griffith Joyner's coach and is now her husband. (Read more about Flo-Jo on page 32!)

Cool Credits

➤ Olympic silver medal, heptathlon, 1984
➤ *Track & Field* Athlete of the Year, 1986
➤ Jesse Owens Award, 1986
➤ Sullivan Award (best amateur athlete), 1986
➤ Olympic gold medals, heptathlon and long jump, 1988
➤ Olympic bronze medal, long jump, 1992

Birthday Beat
March 3, 1962

Vital Stats
➤ Height: 5'10"
➤ Weight: 150
➤ Birthplace: East St. Louis, Illinois
➤ Current residence: Long Beach, California

➤ In her spare time: loves to read (but doesn't have much spare time since she married her coach, Bob Kersee)
➤ Goal for the future: to become a sportscaster
➤ Named after: the late Jacqueline Kennedy Onassis

Jackie Joyner-Kersee
3261 Delta
Long Beach, CA 90810

43

Jim Kelly

Birthday Beat
February 14, 1960

Vital Stats
➤ Height: 6'3"
➤ Weight: 218
➤ Birthplace: East Brady, Pennsylvania
➤ Current residences: East Brady, Pennsylvania, and Orchard Park, New York
➤ Nicknames: Country, Machine-Gun
➤ College: University of Miami
➤ In his spare time: likes to hunt, fish, go camping, watch basketball and hockey, and play softball
➤ Favorite food: anything Mexican
➤ Childhood idols: Hall of Fame QBs Joe Namath and Terry Bradshaw

So You Want to Know—
About Jim Kelly's academic career? Though Jim left college early to sign a professional football contract, he returned to the University of Miami during the off-season and, in 1988, earned his bachelor's degree in business management.

▼▼▼▼▼▼▼▼▼▼▼▼▼▼▼▼▼▼▼▼

*I*t isn't easy to bounce back after losing the Super Bowl three years in a row, but Jim Kelly is one tough quarterback. He once said he didn't want to play in Buffalo because "you can't be a great quarterback in snow and thirty-mile-an-hour winds." But he hasn't let the freezing New York weather bother him or his performance. He helped pioneer the "no-huddle" offense and led the Bills to becoming a perennial winner. Jim has regularly completed more than sixty percent of his pass attempts and has racked up almost 20,000 yards in his NFL career so far.

Cool Credits

➤ Led Miami Hurricanes to their best season and a national ranking
➤ Was top quarterback in United States Football League (a now defunct pro football league)

➤ Third highest rated passer in NFL history (1992)
➤ Led Buffalo Bills to four consecutive AFC titles, 1991–1994
➤ Pro Bowl team, 1986, 1988, 1990, 1991, 1992, 1993

Jim Kelly
7324 Southwest Freeway 280
Houston, TX 77074

Nancy Kerrigan

■ ■ ■ ■ ■ ■ ■ ■ ■ ■ ■ ■ ■

*S*he has been skating since the age of six, and not just figure skating, either. When her two brothers challenged her to play hockey, she didn't mind getting the occasional black eye. Unlike many Olympic-bound skaters, Nancy did not move away from home to find the right coach. She trained near her family in Massachusetts. Win or lose, her family has always been there for her, giving her strength. When Nancy was attacked during the U.S. Nationals, Nancy's family rallied around her and gave her the strength to recover and come within one-tenth of one point of a gold medal in the 1994 Winter Olympics.

Vital Stats

➤ Height: 5'4"
➤ Weight: 115
➤ Birthplace: Woburn, Massachusetts
➤ Current residence: Stoneham, Massachusetts

➤ In her spare time: likes shopping, reading, listening to relaxation tapes, and studying
➤ Her greatest wish: for her mother, who's blind, to be able to see her skate

Birthday Beat
October 13, 1969

Cool Credits

➤ Placed third in U.S. Championships, 1991
➤ Placed third in World Championships, 1991
➤ Trophy Lalique, third place, 1991
➤ Placed first in Nations Cup, 1991
➤ Olympic bronze medal, 1992
➤ Olympic silver medal, 1994

So You Want to Know—

About Nancy's acting debut? In 1988, Nancy appeared in a Coca-Cola commercial playing the part of a Russian figure skater who meets an American hockey player in a skating rink.

Nancy Kerrigan
U.S. Figure Skating Association
20 First St.
Colorado Springs, CO 80906

Julie Krone

❑ ❑ ❑ ❑ ❑ ❑ ❑ ❑ ❑ ❑ ❑ ❑ ❑ ❑ ❑ ❑ ❑ ❑

*T*wenty-five years ago there was no such thing as a female race-horse jockey. Today, Julie Krone not only rides against men, she beats them, and she is considered one of the best jockeys in the world. Her rise to the top of horse racing has not been easy. Early in her career she was thrown from a horse during a race and broke her back. She came back, though, and when other jockeys challenged her, she proved to be tougher than they thought. One jockey pulled the reins from her hands just as she was about to cross the finish line, but Julie managed to keep her balance, stay on the horse, and win!

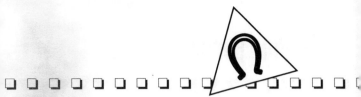

Vital Stats

➤ Height: 4'10½"
➤ Weight: 100
➤ Birthplace: Benton Harbor, Michigan
➤ Current residence: Cherry Hill, New Jersey
➤ In her spare time: loves skiing, lifting weights, doing acrobatics
➤ Interesting pastime: memorizes song lyrics

Cool Credits

➤ First woman ever to win four races in one day at a New York track
➤ Captured all-time record for wins among female jockeys (1,205), 1987
➤ Fourth leading rider (male or female), 1988
➤ Rode two long shots to victory in the Maryland Million Dollar Show main event

So You Want to Know—

About Julie's early riding days? When she was only two years old, Julie's mother put her on a horse and, without any training, she pulled the reins and rode it around. She got so good at riding that by the time she was fifteen years old, she was offered a job as a rider in a circus, which she turned down.

➤ Won the Belmont Stakes, making her the first woman ever to win a Triple Crown race, 1993

Birthday Beat

July 24, 1963

Julie Krone
95 Tennessee Ave.
Long Beach, NY 11561

Mario Lemieux

▼▼▼▼▼▼▼▼▼▼▼▼▼▼▼▼▼▼▼▼▼

Mario has been skating since he was old enough to walk and playing professional hockey since he was fifteen. At six feet four inches, he is bigger than the average hockey player, though he has the agility of a much smaller man and is very difficult to stop. When he joined the NHL, he chose the number 66 because it's Wayne Gretzky's number upside down. And, since hitting the NHL ice, Mario has turned many of his opponents upside down.

So You Want to Know—

How Mario learned to speak English? He's from the French-speaking province, Quebec, in Canada. So when he came to play for the Pitts-burgh Penguins in 1984, Mario knew very little English. He says that he learned English from watching soap operas!

Vital Stats

➤ Height: 6'4"
➤ Weight: 210
➤ Shoots: right-handed
➤ Birthplace: Montreal, Quebec (Canada)
➤ In his spare time: plays golf and video games, watches television
➤ Opening day: scored a goal on the very first shot he ever took in the NHL
➤ Fashion flair: Mario was named Pittsburgh's Dapper Man of the Year in 1986 and 1989!
➤ Nickname: The Magnificent

Cool Credits

➤ Calder Memorial Trophy (best rookie in NHL), 1985

➤ NHL scoring champion, 1988, 1989, 1992

➤ Hart Trophy (NHL Most Valuable Player), 1988

➤ Eight-time NHL all-star

➤ Only player ever to score one of each type of goal in one game (even strength, power play, short handed, penalty shot, and empty net goals), December 31, 1988

Birthday Beat

October 5, 1965

Mario Lemieux
2370 One PPG Place, Suite 1900
Pittsburgh, PA 15222

Carl Lewis

■ ■ ■ ■ ■ ■ ■ ■ ■ ■ ■ ■ ■ ■ ■

Vital Stats

➤ Height: 6'2"
➤ Weight: 180
➤ Birthplace:
Birmingham, Alabama
➤ Current residence:
Houston, Texas
➤ In his spare time:
plays cello, plays with his
dogs, shops, and collects
crystal
➤ Favorite slogan: "Life
has no finish line."

So You Want to Know—

Some of Carl's other
talents? He was draft-
ed by the Chicago
Bulls to play basket-
ball and by the
Dallas Cowboys to
play football, but he
declined both offers.
He also cowrote and
performed a song
called "Going
for the Gold,"
which came
out around
the time of
the 1984
Olympics. In
1987, this
talented guy
also put out
an album
called
*Break It
Up*, which
was very
popular
in parts
of
Europe.

*H*e is the most dominating track-and-field star since Jesse Owens. Carl Lewis was the fastest human and the longest jumper throughout much of the 1980s, during which time he captured six Olympic gold medals. But what distinguishes him from all others even more are his actions when younger runners and jumpers begin to eclipse his greatness. He does not give up. Carl has let the competition inspire him to push himself even farther.

Cool Credits

➤ Sullivan Award (best amateur athlete), 1981
➤ Olympic gold medal 100 meters, 1984, 1988
➤ Olympic gold medal 200 meters, 1984
➤ Olympic gold medal 4x100-meter relay, 1984, 1992
➤ Olympic gold medal long jump, 1984, 1988, 1992
➤ World record, 100 meters (9.86 seconds), 1991
➤ First track-and-field athlete since Jesse Owens to win four Olympic gold medals during a single Olympics

Birthday Beat

July 1, 1961

Carl Lewis
1801 Ocean Park Blvd., Suite 112
Santa Monica, CA 90405

Karl Malone

▢ ▢ ▢ ▢ ▢ ▢ ▢ ▢ ▢ ▢ ▢ ▢ ▢ ▢ ▢ ▢ ▢

When he came out of college, a lot of NBA teams didn't think Karl Malone was ready for the professional game. They were wrong. In only a few years he has become a perennial all-star, all-NBA selection, and is considered by some to be the best power forward in the game. He is famous for his fastbreak drives. When he goes to the basket, he doesn't try to spin around or fake defenders. He goes right at them, challenging them to stand there and take a charge, and most of the time defenders clear the way. Karl is a great competitor who loves to win, and he hates to come out of a game, no matter how tired he is.

So You Want to Know—

How Karl built up his strength? When he was a teenager, Karl wrestled 200-pound hogs on the farm where his family lived.

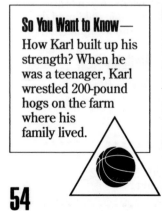

Cool Credits

➤ All-rookie team, 1986
➤ Western Conference all-star, 1987–1994
➤ All-star game Most Valuable Player, 1989
➤ All-NBA first team, 1989–1993
➤ Olympic gold medal, 1992

Vital Stats

➤ Height: 6'9"
➤ Weight: 256
➤ Birthplace: Summerfield, Louisiana
➤ Current residences: Salt Lake City, Utah, and Dallas, Texas
➤ In his spare time: enjoys horseback riding, hunting, fishing, going to amusement parks, watching boxing and football, and truck driving

➤ Nickname: The Mailman
➤ Favorite food: soul food
➤ Inspiration: his mother, who used to run a forklift in order to earn money to feed Karl and his brothers and sisters

Birthday Beat

July 24, 1963

Karl Malone
c/o Utah Jazz
The Delta Center
301 West South Temple
Salt Lake City, UT 84101

Mark McGwire

Cool Credits

➤ Rookie of the Year, 1987
➤ First player ever to hit thirty or more home runs during his first four seasons in the majors, 1987–1990
➤ World Series team victory, 1989
➤ American League Golden Glove Award (best fielder at first base in the league), 1990

So You Want to Know—

How graceful Mark is off the field? In a 1990 Oakland Ballet production of *The Nutcracker*, Mark danced the part of a toy soldier!

Birthday Beat

October 1, 1963

Growing up in Southern California, Mark McGwire was always a shy kid. When he was in school, he dreaded the possibility that the teacher might call on him. But out on the baseball field, he was always comfortable. And now playing for the Oakland A's in the big leagues, with millions watching, Mark isn't the least bit shy about knocking a hanging curve ball over the center field wall. He is one of baseball's great sluggers and has also become one of the best-fielding first basemen. But best of all, he is one of the nicest and most easily approachable superstars in baseball— Mark appreciates his fans as much as they appreciate him.

Vital Stats

➤ Height: 6'5"
➤ Weight: 225
➤ Birthplace: Pomona, California
➤ Current residence: Alamo, California

➤ In his spare time: loves the movies, TV news shows, and playing golf
➤ Favorite foods: steak, chicken, and pasta
➤ Family: Brother Dan is an NFL quarterback with the Seattle Seahawks.

Mark McGwire
P.O. Box 2220
Oakland, CA 94621

Shannon Miller

■ ■ ■ ■ ■ ■ ■ ■ ■ ■ ■ ■ ■ ■ ■

*W*hen the U.S. women's gymnastics team went to Barcelona for the 1992 Olympics, everyone thought Kim Zmeskal would be the big winner. Petite Shannon Miller surprised everyone by winning five medals, including a team bronze, which she was instrumental in earning. She is a tough competitor who is never afraid to take risks. Shannon's Olympic performance was especially impressive considering that, only months earlier, she had a tiny screw put inside her arm to repair a dislocated left elbow.

Cool Credits

➤ U.S. Nationals third place vault, 1991
➤ U.S. Nationals first place balance beam, 1991
➤ World Championships second place team, 1991
➤ World Championships second place uneven bars, 1991
➤ U.S. Olympic Trials first place all-around, 1992
➤ Olympic silver medals all-around, balance beam, 1992
➤ Olympic bronze medal uneven bars, floor exercises, team competition, 1992

Birthday Beat

March 10, 1977

Vital Stats

➤ Height: 4'9"
➤ Weight: 79
➤ Birthplace: Rolla, Missouri
➤ Current residence: Edmond, Oklahoma
➤ In her spare time: likes to roller-skate and travel
➤ Pets: has a horse, a dog, some gerbils, fish, and a cat named Gizmo
➤ Favorite sport besides her own: basketball
➤ Favorite food: pizza
➤ Favorite TV show: "Roseanne"
➤ Favorite subject in school: algebra

So You Want to Know—

How Shannon helps her father in his job? Her father is a physics professor at the University of Oklahoma. He uses videotapes of Shannon performing gymnastics routines in order to demonstrate the laws of physics to his students.

Shannon Miller
U.S. Gymnastics Federation
Ten American Plaza
201 South Capital Ave., Suite 300
Indianapolis, IN 46225

Joe Montana

*S*ome have called Joe Montana the greatest quarterback ever. He is at least in the Top 3 by all accounts. When Joe Montana is in uniform, you can never count his team out of a game. His two-minute drill (his ability to score quickly in the final minutes of a game) is legendary. In recent years, he has been stricken with the kind of injuries that end players' careers, but Joe keeps coming back and remaining one of the premier quarterbacks in the NFL. He has nothing left to prove. He just loves to play, to compete, and to win.

Cool Credits

➤ Highest regular season completion percentage (64%) in NFL history, 1989
➤ Highest QB rating (93.4) of all NFL quarterbacks
➤ Led his team to Super Bowl wins, 1982, 1985, 1989, 1990
➤ Most yards passing (357) in a single Super Bowl, 1989
➤ Super Bowl Most Valuable Player, 1982, 1985, 1990
➤ Most Super Bowl yards passing (1,142) of any QB in NFL history
➤ Most Super Bowl touchdowns (11) of any QB in NFL history

Vital Stats

➤ Height: 6'2"
➤ Weight: 195
➤ Birthplace: New Eagle, Pennsylvania
➤ Current residence: Palo Alto, California

So You Want to Know—

About Joe's famous "chicken soup" game? Playing in the 1979 Cotton Bowl as quarterback for Notre Dame, Joe got so cold that he ended up in the locker room with hypothermia. The team trainer had to feed him hot soup until his temperature was up to 97 degrees; then Joe came back on the field and led an incredible come-back, capped with a last-second pass for a one-point victory.

➤ In his spare time: enjoys wine tasting, playing basketball, vacationing with his family

➤ Charity tosses: Every time Joe throws a touchdown pass, he and his wife, Jennifer, donate $200 to the Crippled Children's Society of Santa Clara, located in California.

Birthday Beat
June 11, 1956

• •

Joe Montana
c/o International Management Group
One Erieview Plaza, Suite 1300
Cleveland, OH 44144

• •

Warren Moon

*E*ver since the 1950s, professional football has been integrated. There have been running backs, linemen, receivers, and defensive backs of all races and colors. But the quarterback, the team leader, was always white. In fact, this was often true at the collegiate level. Warren Moon helped to change all that. When he graduated from high school as an all-American high school quarterback, he was offered football scholarships by several big-time universities. But they all wanted him to play a different position. He refused. He went to a junior college and proved himself as a viable quarterback. He helped break the color barrier at the major university level at the University of Washington, and then at the pro level with the Houston Oilers.

Cool Credits

➤ High school all-American, 1974
➤ AFC Pro Bowl starting quarterback, 1989
➤ AFC Pro Bowl starting quarterback, 1990
➤ AFC Most Valuable Player, 1990
➤ Associated Press NFL Offensive Player of the Year, 1990

Vital Stats

➤ Height: 6'3"
➤ Weight: 220
➤ Birthplace: Los Angeles, California
➤ Current residence: Sugar Land, Texas
➤ In his spare time: likes to fish, swim, play basketball, watch all sports, go to concerts (especially Luther Vandross and Phil Collins), and see plays and musicals

So You Want to Know—

Where Warren first played pro ball? His first six years in professional football weren't in Houston or anywhere in the United States. His first contract was with the Edmonton Eskimos of the Canadian Football League. In fact, Warren is the only quarterback ever to throw for more than 20,000 yards both in the CFL and the NFL.

➤ Favorite food: chicken
➤ Nickname: Dad

Birthday Beat
November 18, 1956

Warren Moon
6910 Fannin
Houston, TX 77030

Shaquille O'Neal

■ ■ ■ ■ ■ ■ ■ ■ ■ ■ ■ ■ ■

*H*e's only a rookie, but in his first season in the NBA, Shaquille O'Neal has proven to be one of the league's dominant players. He made the Orlando Magic the most improved team in basketball with his great strength, athleticism, and versatility. This guy used to hate being so tall because kids in school thought he was dumb and had been kept back a grade or two. But now he's certainly found a way to make his height pay off. Keep an eye on Shaq—he may turn out to be one of the greatest basketball players of all time.

Cool Credits

➤ First team NCAA all-American, 1992
➤ First draft pick NBA, 1992
➤ NBA all-star, 1993, 1994
➤ NBA Rookie of the Year, 1993

Vital Stats

➤ Height: 7'1"
➤ Weight: 301

➤ Birthplace: Newark, New Jersey
➤ Current residence: Islesworth, Florida
➤ College: Louisiana State University
➤ In his spare time: collects and drives cars, goes to amusement parks
➤ Shoe size: twenty-four (big enough to pour four 12-ounce cans of soda into)
➤ Nickname: Shaq ("Shack")
➤ Number of backboards he destroyed during his rookie season: two

Birthday Beat
March 6, 1972

So You Want to Know—

About the *second* Shaquille? When he was in college at Louisiana State University, Shaq discovered that a couple had named their baby son Shaquille O'Neal Long in honor of their favorite player. Shaq got in his car and drove halfway across the state of Louisiana to have his picture taken with his namesake.

Shaquille O'Neal
c/o Orlando Magic
Orlando Arena
One Magic Place
Orlando, FL 32801

Scottie Pippen

Birthday Beat
September 25, 1965

Cool Credits
➤ All-star, 1991–1994
➤ All-NBA second team, 1992, 1993
➤ NBA Championship, 1991–1993
➤ Olympic gold medal, 1992

So You Want to Know—
About one of Scottie's favorite neighbors? Scottie lives right next door to the Bulls' other starting forward, Horace Grant. In fact, the two are very good friends on and off the court.

□ □ □ □ □ □ □ □ □ □ □ □ □ □ □ □ □ □ □

*A*s a kid growing up in a small town in Arkansas, Scottie Pippen watched televised basketball games with awe. Whenever he saw Julius Erving, known as Dr. J., swoop across the key for a resounding dunk or hang in the air and palm the ball, Scottie would dream of a basketball career of his own. Now Scottie does all those things and more. He can handle the ball, pass, shoot from outside, or take the ball to the basket. He's a good defender and rebounder, and he works hard to win. Scottie is the Chicago Bulls' "Iron Man." For three years in a row, he played all eighty-two games in each season.

Vital Stats

➤ Height: 6'7"
➤ Weight: 225
➤ Birthplace: Hamburg, Arkansas
➤ College: University of Central Arkansas

➤ Current residence: Northbrook, Illinois
➤ In his spare time: plays with his son and their dogs, drives powerboats
➤ Nickname: Pip
➤ Favorite food: steak

Scottie Pippen
980 N. Michigan Ave., Suite 1600
Chicago, IL 60611

Kirby Puckett

▼▼▼▼▼▼▼▼▼▼▼▼▼▼▼▼▼▼▼

*H*e looks more like a football halfback than a baseball center fielder, but don't let that fool you. Kirby Puckett is one of the best all-around players in modern baseball history. He can run the bases, hit home runs, field, and get on base (his batting average has been over .300 five of his eight seasons in the majors). Kirby's energy and determination help motivate his teammates to play their best. They always know they can count on him for a clutch hit, a comeback home run, or a diving catch to save the game.

So You Want to Know—
What Kirby does to avoid bad luck?
Kirby is superstitious about baseball. When he runs on and off the field, he is careful not to step on the first or third baselines—just in case it might bring bad luck.

Cool Credits
➤ American League Golden Glove Award, 1985–1990
➤ Helped Twins to World Series wins, 1987, 1991
➤ Batted league-leading .356, 1988
➤ ALCS Most Valuable Player, 1991
➤ All-star team, 1990–1993

Birthday Beat
March 14, 1961

Vital Stats

➤ Height: 5'8"
➤ Weight: 220
➤ Birthplace: Chicago, Illinois
➤ Current residence: Edina, Minnesota
➤ In his spare time: relaxes with his wife and daughter, plays basketball, listens to jazz music
➤ Favorite foods: chicken and catfish
➤ Nicknames: Puck, Toy Cannon, Human Fire Hydrant, Spark Plug
➤ Childhood idol: Ernie Banks

Kirby Puckett
c/o Minnesota Twins
501 Chicago Ave. South
Minneapolis, MN 55415

Jerry Rice

Many experts as well as defensive backs consider Jerry Rice to be the most dangerous receiver in professional football. He has burned his share of defenders trying to cover him one-on-one or even two-on-one. He can run a short pattern for a sure first down, or go deep for long yardage. He is one of the most difficult receivers to tackle and has become almost legendary for turning a five- or ten-yard pass into a fifty- or sixty-yard touchdown. In the eight seasons he has been with the 49ers, Jerry has helped make them the most dominant team in football.

Cool Credits

➤ NFL Most Valuable Player, 1986
➤ Super Bowl victories, 1985, 1989, 1990
➤ Super Bowl Most Valuable Player, 1989
➤ All-pro, 1986, 1987, 1988

Birthday Beat

October 13, 1962

Vital Stats

➤ Height: 6'2"
➤ Weight: 200
➤ Birthplace: Crawford, Mississippi
➤ Current residence: Redwood Shores, California
➤ In his spare time: listens to soul music, goes dancing with his wife
➤ Nickname: Flash-80

So You Want to Know—

How Jerry got interested in football? One day in high school, Jerry was cutting class. When the principal saw him, Jerry ran. The principal was so impressed with his quickness that he recommended Rice to the high school football coach. The rest is history!

➤ Training technique: practices catching with bricks
➤ Favorite foods: pasta and fish

Jerry Rice
c/o San Francisco 49ers
4949 Centennial Blvd.
Santa Clara, CA 95054

Cal Ripken, Jr.

□ □ □ □ □ □ □ □ □ □ □ □ □ □ □ □ □

*H*e is one of the greatest all-around shortstops ever to play baseball. At six feet four inches, Cal Ripken, Jr., is also the tallest full-time shortstop in the history of major league baseball. You might think this would make it difficult to field grounders, since his arms are farther from the ground than the average infielder's, but he can snag ground balls with the best. He can execute the double play as well as anyone. In fact, he is one of the best defensive infielders in the game. He can hit for power or just to get on base. And Cal is an Iron Man—he never gets injured or misses a game—second all-time in consecutive games played, to Lou Gehrig, the original Iron Man.

Cool Credits

➤ Rookie of the Year, 1982
➤ American League Most Valuable Player 1983, 1991
➤ Golden Glove Award (best fielder in the league), 1991

➤ Second longest streak for consecutive games played, 1870 as of the beginning of the 1994 season
➤ Record for most consecutive errorless games by a shortstop (95)
➤ Record for most home runs (289) of any career shortstop, as of 1993 season
➤ All-star team, 1983–1993

So You Want to Know—

About the other Ripken baseball stars? Cal's father, Cal Ripken, Sr., was a minor league catcher for the Orioles back in the 1950s. The older Ripken's catching career was ended by a shoulder injury in 1961. He remained in baseball and eventually became the Orioles manager at the same time that Cal Jr. was the star shortstop and his younger brother Billy Ripken was the second baseman.

Vital Stats

➤ Height: 6'4"
➤ Weight: 218
➤ Birthplace: Havre de Grace, Maryland
➤ Current residence: Reisterstown, Maryland
➤ In his spare time: plays basketball and racquetball

Birthday Beat

August 24, 1960

Cal Ripken, Jr.
c/o The Tufton Group
333 Camden St.
Baltimore, MD 21201

David Robinson

David Robinson didn't always dream of becoming a professional basketball player. He wanted to be an engineer. As a kid, he loved to take things apart and then put them back together. He didn't play organized basketball until high school. A few years later, he was the starting center for the navy team, and soon became the best collegiate player in the country, receiving the NCAA Player of the Year for 1987. Now David is one of the most dominating players in the NBA, but he still continues his intellectual interests off the court.

Cool Credits

➤ NCAA Player of the Year, 1987
➤ Olympic bronze medal, 1988
➤ Rookie of the Year, 1990
➤ Olympic gold medal, 1992
➤ All-NBA first team, 1991, 1992

Vital Stats

➤ Height: 7'1"
➤ Weight: 235
➤ Birthplace: Key West, Florida
➤ Current residence: San Antonio, Texas
➤ College: Naval Academy, Annapolis, Maryland
➤ Nickname: The Admiral

Birthday Beat

August 6, 1965

So You Want to Know—

How David's height got him out of the navy? Because he was in the navy, David Robinson was not allowed to play pro ball after his senior year of college. Instead, he was supposed to spend five years as a naval officer aboard a ship. But because he had grown to be more than seven feet tall, the secretary of the navy ruled that Robinson could no longer fit into most naval vessels and planes. He was given a desk job instead, which allowed him to join the NBA in two years.

David Robinson
c/o San Antonio Spurs
600 East Market St., Suite 102
San Antonio, TX 78205

Nolan Ryan

Any doctor can tell you that the natural motion of a human arm is underhand, and that people were not designed to throw ninety-mile-an-hour fastballs by the hundreds, day after day. That is why most baseball pitchers don't last more than ten years. But Texas Ranger Nolan Ryan pitched in the major leagues for more than twenty-five years and struck out men half his age. Some baseball fans consider him the eighth wonder of the world, and the entire baseball world was saddened when he retired in 1993.

Vital Stats

➤ Height: 6'2"
➤ Weight: 210
➤ Birthplace: Refugio, Texas
➤ Current residence: Alvin, Texas
➤ In his spare time: likes horseback riding, ranching
➤ Other career: runs the Danbury Bank in Danbury, Texas
➤ Nicknames: Nolie, Tex, The Ryan Express

➤ Special warm-ups: lifts dumbbells, throws a football

Birthday Beat

January 31, 1947

Cool Credits

➤ Holds record for most no-hitters (six as of the end of the 1992 season)
➤ Holds record for career strikeouts (5,668 as of the end of the 1992 season)
➤ Best national league ERA, 1981 (1.69), 1987 (2.76)

➤ Most strikeouts in the American League, 1972 (329), 1973 (383), 1974 (367), 1976 (327), 1977 (341), 1978 (260), 1979 (223), 1989 (301), 1990 (232)

➤ Most strikeouts in the National League, 1987 (270), 1988 (228)

So You Want to Know—

How baseball brought Nolan and his wife together? He met his wife, Ruth, when he was just a kid playing Little League baseball. She used to go to the games with her big sister, and when she saw Nolan pitch, she thought he was cute. Now they have two sons and a daughter, who all played Little League themselves.

Nolan Ryan
719 Dezzo Dr.
Alvin, TX 77511

Gabriela Sabatini

So You Want to Know—

Gabriela's little-known credit? She was the first female athlete ever to have a line of perfume named after her. It's called *Gaby*.

Vital Stats

➤ Height: 5'8"
➤ Weight: 130
➤ Hits: right-handed
➤ Birthplace: Buenos Aires, Argentina
➤ Current residences: Buenos Aires, as well as Key Biscayne, Florida
➤ In her spare time: goes to the beach, plays guitar, dances, rides a hot pink motorcycle
➤ Nickname: Gaby

□ □ □ □ □ □ □ □ □ □ □ □ □ □ □ □ □ □

*S*he was fourteen years old when she moved from Argentina to Florida to study tennis full-time. That year she entered the eighteen-and-under French Open and won. A year later, at fifteen, she became a professional tennis player. Immediately Gabriela Sabatini made her presence known, defeating six top-ranked players during the first month. It wasn't long before she was one of the top women tennis players in the world. Gabriela can do it all with a devastating serve and the ability to mix volleys, lobs, drop shots, and baseliners with an awesome topspin.

Cool Credits

➤ Eighteen-and-under French Open winner, 1986
➤ U.S. Open winner, 1990
➤ Wimbledon finalist, 1991
➤ Pan-Pacific Open winner, 1992
➤ Number three world ranking, 1992

Birthday Beat

May 16, 1970

Gabriela Sabatini
ProServ Inc.
1101 West Wilson Blvd., Suite 1800
Arlington, VA 22209

Barry Sanders

He isn't big, weighing about fifty pounds less than the average 250-pound lineman. But he is fast, quick, and, most of all, tough. Throughout most of his childhood, he was smaller than the other boys. In fact, high school football coaches felt he was just too small to be an effective running back. He proved them wrong with a 1,417-yard senior year. Most college coaches also felt he was too small, but someone at Oklahoma State believed in him. They made him a backup for two years. Then, when they gave him the chance to start, he turned out to be the best running back in the NCAA! Now Barry is in the NFL, playing for the Detroit Lions and making believers out of fans, teammates, and especially the defenses who have attempted to tackle him.

Cool Credits

➤ Oklahoma State record, fifty-six college career touchdowns, 1988
➤ Five touchdowns in the Holiday Bowl, 1988

➤ Heisman Trophy winner (best player in college football), 1988
➤ Led NFC in rushing, 1989 (1,470 yards), 1990 (1,304 yards)
➤ NFL all-rookie team selection, 1989

➤ NFL all pro selection, 1990, 1991
➤ Led NFL in total yards from scrimmage (1,855 yards), 1991

Vital Stats

➤ Height: 5'8"
➤ Weight: 203
➤ Birthplace: Wichita, Kansas
➤ Current residence: Rochester Hills, Michigan
➤ College: attended Oklahoma State University
➤ 40-yard-dash speed: 4.27 seconds
➤ Amount of weight he can squat lift: 557 pounds
➤ In his spare time: watches and plays basketball, reads
➤ Favorite food: pasta
➤ Idol growing up: Muhammad Ali

Birthday Beat

July 16, 1968

So You Want to Know—

How generous Barry is? When he heard that a supermarket in his hometown was about to go out of business, leaving many poor and elderly people without a place to buy food, Barry stepped in and bought the market to keep it open.

Barry Sanders
1200 Featherstone Rd.
Pontiac, MI 48057

Summer Sanders

■ ■ ■ ■ ■ ■ ■ ■ ■ ■ ■ ■ ■ ■ ■

*W*hen Summer Sanders was two years old, her parents made her take swimming lessons so she would be safe in the family's pool. Summer didn't seem to enjoy swimming at all, until one day when she took off the inflatable wings and kept herself afloat. That was the beginning of a very successful swimming career. In 1988, Summer entered the U.S. Olympic trials, not to win but to improve by competing against the top American swimmers. She came within .27 of a second of making the U.S. Olympic team. Four years later, Summer was heading for the Olympics, and when she returned with three medals, there was little doubt that she had become one of the top swimmers in the world.

Birthday Beat
October 13, 1972

Cool Credits

➤ U.S. Nationals first place 200-meter individual medley, 1990
➤ U.S. Spring Nationals first place 100-meter butterfly, 1991
➤ World Championships first place 200-meter butterfly, 1991
➤ Pan Pacific Championships first place 200-meter butterfly, 200-meter individual medley, and 400-meter individual medley, 1991
➤ Olympic gold medal 200-meter butterfly, silver medal 200-meter individual medley, and bronze medal 400-meter individual medley, 1992

Vital Stats

➤ Height: 5'9"
➤ Weight: 125

➤ Birthplace and current residence: Roseville, California
➤ In her spare time: follows basketball (especially the Chicago Bulls), enjoys waterskiing and bungee jumping
➤ Nickname: Scummer

So You Want to Know—

Summer's favorite athlete? She's a big Michael Jordan fan! In fact, when traveling to a swim meet, Summer has been known to carry along an Air Jordan poster and stick it to a wall with toothpaste so that her idol can watch her swim to victory.

Summer Sanders
U.S. Swimming
One Olympic Plaza
Colorado Springs, CO 80909

Monica Seles

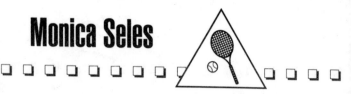

*S*he learned tennis from her father, who used to draw a cartoon cat on tennis balls and tell her that a tennis player has to attack an opponent the way a cat attacks a mouse. And that is the way she plays. She goes all out and is always on the offensive, wearing her opponent down. So far, this style has worked. As a professional, Monica has won a remarkable ninety percent of her matches. However, she is more than just a winner; she is a courageous survivor, returning to near top form after being brutally attacked during a match by a man with a knife.

Vital Stats

➤ Height: 5'9½"
➤ Weight: 130
➤ Birthplace: Novi Sad, Yugoslavia
➤ Current residences: Sarasota, Florida, and Los Angeles, California
➤ In her spare time: likes playing basketball, juggling, swimming, shopping, and reading
➤ Favorite off-the-court attire: jeans
➤ Pet: a Yorkshire terrier named Astro
➤ Favorite singer: Madonna

Cool Credits

➤ Named Yugoslavia's Sportswoman of the Year at age eleven, 1984
➤ Youngest woman (sixteen years old) ever to win the French Open, 1990

➤ Youngest woman (seventeen years old) ever to win the Australian Open, 1991

➤ Youngest tennis player (seventeen years old) ever ranked number one in the world, 1991

➤ First woman in fifty years to win the French Open three years in a row, 1990–1992

➤ Australian Open winner, 1993

Birthday Beat

December 2, 1973

So You Want to Know—

Why Monica doesn't mind giving autographs? As a child, Monica tried to get an autograph from a professional tennis player and was rudely turned down. She still remembers how that felt, so she tries never to say no to a fan with pen and paper.

Monica Seles
c/o International Management Group
22 East 71st St.
New York, NY 10021

Jenny Thompson

▼▼▼▼▼▼▼▼▼▼▼▼▼▼▼▼▼▼▼▼

*O*lympic gold medalist Jenny Thompson grew up in New Hampshire, which is not exactly the most likely place for a swimmer to develop. New Hampshire is cold most of the year, too cold for outdoor swimming. Jenny did most of her laps in a small pool inside a building that had been converted from a municipal garage. But as surprised as Jenny has been by her success, it was not accidental. Her rigorous training included bodybuilding for arm and leg strength. In fact, her workouts earned her the nickname "Lou," after Lou Ferrigno, the actor who played the Incredible Hulk on television.

Birthday Beat
February 26, 1973

Vital Stats
➤ Height: 5'10"
➤ Weight: 155
➤ Birthplace: Danvers, Massachusetts
➤ Current residence: Dover, New Hampshire
➤ In her spare time: likes to play pickup games of basketball and to roller-skate
➤ Favorite foods: Ben & Jerry's Cookie Dough or Chunky Monkey ice cream

So You Want to Know—
What Jenny collects? Anything with the American flag on it! Not just your typical American flag items—like pins or stamps—but strange items, such as American flag wastebaskets, rugs, and telephones.

Cool Credits
➤ Pan American Games, first place 50-meter freestyle, 1987, 1989
➤ U.S. Nationals, first place 50-meter freestyle, 1990
➤ Olympic gold medals 4x100-meter freestyle relay and 4x100-meter medley relay, 1992

Jenny Thompson
U.S. Swimming
One Olympic Plaza
Colorado Springs, CO 80909

Dominique Wilkins

■ ■ ■ ■ ■ ■ ■ ■ ■ ■ ■ ■ ■ ■

*H*e was born in France and given the French name, Jacques Dominique Wilkins. Dominique's family was living in France because his father, a U.S. Army sergeant, was stationed there. In France, the big sport is soccer (which they call football), and Dominique might have become a world-class soccer player except that, when he was four years old, Dominique's family moved to Atlanta where he learned to play basketball. Now he is known throughout America, as well as France and most of the rest of the world, as one of the greatest basketball players and scorers anyone has ever seen. His offensive moves, four-foot vertical leaping ability, spinning shots, and tomahawk dunks have made him one of the most entertaining athletes in the world to watch.

Birthday Beat

January 12, 1960

Vital Stats

➤ Height: 6'8"
➤ Weight: 215
➤ Birthplace: Paris, France
➤ Current residence: Atlanta, Georgia
➤ Loves: playing marbles, eating soul food

> Nicknames: The Human Highlight Film, Nique
> Nique's pad: a 14,000-square-foot house with seven bedrooms and a movie theater

So You Want to Know—

How Dominique practices his shooting accuracy for the court? He shoots marbles and is an expert player. Just ask his brother, Gerald Wilkins, who has played basketball for the Cleveland Cavs and the New York Knicks. Gerald has been shooting marbles against Nique his whole life and has never beaten him!

Cool Credits

> Fifth highest career playoff scoring average in NBA history (26.1 points)
> Sixth highest career regular-season scoring average in NBA history (26.2 points)
> Seventeenth highest all-time NBA scorer
> All-star slam-dunk champion, 1985, 1990
> All-NBA first team, 1986
> All-NBA second team, 1987, 1988, 1991

Dominique Wilkins
5775 Peach Tree Dunwoody Rd., Suite B-130
Atlanta, GA 30342

Katarina Witt

Vital Stats

➤ Height: 5'5"
➤ Weight: 115
➤ Birthplace: Saxony, East Germany
➤ Current residence: Saxony, Unified Germany
➤ In her spare time: loves to drive, travel, and listen to American music
➤ Favorite American composer: George Gershwin
➤ Number of love letters she received after her 1984 Olympic performance: 35,000

So You Want to Know—

About Katarina's second love? Katarina is also an actress. She has been studying acting for many years, which has helped her figure skating performances and gives her something to look forward to once she retires from the ice.

From the time she was in kindergarten, Katarina Witt wanted to skate. The first time she glided across the ice, she knew she wanted to devote herself to the sport. At the age of nine, she was discovered by her country's most successful skating coach, Jutta Müller. When she was only fourteen, Katarina finished tenth in the world championship competition. The next year she came in fifth; and the year after that, in 1982, Katarina won her first European championship and placed second in the world. She was still a teenager when she achieved her ultimate goals in 1984—an Olympic gold and a world championship.

Cool Credits

➤ World Championships, 1984, 1985, 1987, 1988
➤ Olympic gold medal in singles, 1984, 1988

Birthday Beat

December 3, 1965

Katarina Witt
U.S. Figure Skating Association
20 First St.
Colorado Springs, CO 80906

Kristi Yamaguchi

n 1976, Kristi Yamaguchi watched her heroine, figure skater Dorothy Hamill, bring home an Olympic gold. Kristi was five years old then, and just learning to skate. In order to become a world-class skater, she devoted much of her childhood and teenage years to skating, spending an average of five hours a day on the ice. At the beginning of 1992, few expected her to become the preeminent singles skater. Kristi had established herself as a great artistic skater, but many experts felt that she wasn't good enough at the special spinning jumps and other extremely difficult moves. She proved them wrong, combining artistry and athletic ability to dazzle the judges and win a gold medal.

Cool Credits

➤ Up-and-Coming Artistic Athlete of the Year, given by the Women's Sports Foundation, 1988
➤ U.S. Junior Champion in pairs skating, 1986, 1988
➤ World Junior Champion in both pairs and singles skating events, 1988
➤ World Champion in singles, 1991
➤ Winner of both U.S. and World Championships in singles, 1992
➤ Olympic gold medal in singles, 1992

Birthday Beat
July 12, 1971

Vital Stats

➤ Height: 5'0"
➤ Weight: 92
➤ Birthplace: Hayward, California
➤ Current residence: Fremont, California
➤ In her spare time: plays tennis, reads, dances, watches pro football
➤ Overcoming obstacles: was born with club feet, which were corrected by wearing special shoes

So You Want to Know—

Where Kristi gets her inspiration from? Her childhood idol, Dorothy Hamill, is now a friend and fan of Kristi's. In fact, Dorothy visited and encouraged Kristi right before she went on for what was to be her gold medal performance in the 1992 Winter Olympics.

Kristi Yamaguchi
c/o International Management Group
22 E. 71st St.
New York, NY 10021

Steve Young

Vital Stats

➤ Height: 6'2"
➤ Weight: 200
➤ Birthplace: Salt Lake City, Utah
➤ Current residence: Palo Alto, California
➤ In his spare time: attends law school during the off-season, watches baseball, enjoys sailing
➤ College: Brigham Young University
➤ Goals after football: to practice law and get into politics

Cool Credits

➤ NCAA all-American, 1983
➤ Heisman Trophy runner-up, 1983
➤ Super Bowl team victory, 1990
➤ NFL Most Valuable Player, 1993

*I*magine what it must be like to be a very talented quarterback but hardly ever play because the best quarterback of all time is on your team. Would you ask to be traded? Not if you were Steve Young. For seven seasons, Steve was Joe Montana's backup, and in 1992, he proved what a great quarterback he could be. Joe Montana was out the entire season with a back injury and Steve Young became the starting quarterback—and turned out to be one of the best quarterbacks in the league! Now Montana is with the Kansas City Chiefs and the Niners are Steve's team.

So You Want to Know—
About Steve's famous ancestor? Steve Young is the great-great-grandson of Brigham Young, the leader of the Mormon Church of the Latter-Day Saints during the mid-1800s.

Birthday Beat
October 11, 1961

Steve Young
711 Nevada St.
Redwood City, CA 94061

Photo Credits: